# Butterfly Within

Bev
Your Journey has just begun!
Love + Light
Kathy Garbe
"1/2004"

BY
Kathleen Garbe-Modzelewski

# Butterfly Within



Library of Congress Cataloging in Publication Data

**A Harvest Institute Release**

Insight Publishing
P.O. Box 4189
Sevierville, TN 37864

Printed in USA

**Original Cover Art: Christy Garbe**
**Cover Design: Douglas Graphics**

ISBN No. 1-885-640-58-7

# DEDICATION

I would like to dedicate this book to three lovely souls.

One is my teacher, Reverend Stanley Gutt, for through his teaching and love, this book has come forth.

My mentor, Joseph Cipriano, who has stood by me and encouraged me along the way with his enthusiasm and willingness to keep my spirits up when I felt at a low.

To my dear husband and best friend, Michael. I love you and thank you for your patience and understanding along the way and what a journey it has been.

To all three, God bless you all.

## Special Thanks Go Out to Special People

To my daughter, Christy Garbe, who drew from her heart the beautiful, inspirational cover page: The butterfly that lies within every one of us.

To Joanne Vance and Gayle Rexroat, two beautiful friends that have helped me with the typing of my book.

To my husband, Michael, and everyone else that I vented at and talked their ears off—thanks for listening.

To my mother and father, without you I would never have become me. Love from your daughter.

To Lizzy, my special friend and spirit guide. Without her this book would never have been completed.

To the one that accomplished this as a whole, to God, I thank You and love You. We shall share our book with the world!

# INTRODUCTION

Have you ever wondered how or why or maybe even what life is all about?

Life, in general. Everyday things. The way we see it the way we feel about it and the way we wish it was! These thoughts in general are and always will be.

For we are a people of understanding and a willingness to learn. We want to be heard. Yet, are we willing to listen? We want to do, but are we willing to wait? We want what we feel is ours. But, are we willing to give?

These questions make up our lives – yours and mine. They are very simple questions. The answers come back in a very simple form. Are you willing to open up to what it is we have to give to you? This is a story of a coming out.

A celebration of a New World, yet a very Old World. A celebration of a new me, if you will. One in which I would like to share with you. You have heard others talk to you about your angels, guides, and your teachers. Well, I am here to share with you about my guides, my angels and my teachers. I have written this book with the help of my guide. Her name is Elizabeth. You may call her Lizzy. She does not care how you spell it as long as it makes you feel good inside.

She came to me one day to share in a book of knowledge and truth, in its simplest form. To touch on a few of the everyday problems we have in our lives, past and present. To bring together understanding and knowledge to those who are willing to look a little deeper. She comes to me each morning at 8:00 A.M. We have an appointment scheduled. We share, write, and speak to each other. I guess you could call it conversing. I call it sharing time with my friend. For that is how I look at it. You see she explains things to me – the how and why of it; the beginning version, if you will. The knowledge we all need to know and learn, to know we can all learn how to communicate if we wish. These are but a few simple steps of our past, present and future. We must forgive our past and let it go. Live in our present and look forward to the future. Life is one of beauty. There is a love so great it is almost indescribable. If you are interested in this quest, please proceed forward. I'll start at the beginning.

One day while taking a shower I was told I would write a new book and the name would be Butterfly Within. Wow! I was flabbergasted. I got out of the shower and went straight to my husband and told him what I heard. What a beautiful title – Butterfly Within. I sat right down, meditated and went into prayer. I asked for my guide to come to me and help me with our new book. This beautiful guide by the name of Elizabeth came with a sense of humor as you shall see in her writings.

As we started our writing, we shared, and as we began to share, it hit home. I realized for the first time, that I still had not forgiven my past, my pain, and my heartache. I thought I had, but I realized I really had not. Now, I knew how very important it was to let go, forgive, reach out, and give. To be whole once more and to be full of love for myself and for others. For only in this way I can grow to be the person I was intended to be. Through my friend and guide, Lizzy, I have found a peace, wholeness and yet a newness has come about, one in which growth comes. I have stepped out of my cocoon and I have become that Butterfly Within. Please, won't you come and share with us in our adventures of life.

# Preface

## Butterfly Within.

What a beautiful statement. One of truth of each and every one of us. What we need to ask is what and how can we become that butterfly so that we may spring forth from our cocoon and fly into the day with beauty and love. To intermingle with our daily activities. Become one with the Universe. Soar as high as a butterfly can and to become that beautiful tender, wonderful, delicate being. To be one. To be you, to be me, to be free.

# *MY SOUL*

*My soul is free to reach the sky*

*I wonder why this can't be so*

*For all to reach just as high*

*That they to, can reach the sky.*

*-Kathleen Garbe-Modzelewski-*

# Table of Contents

*I wish for all to know that this book has not been edited word for word. For these are the words that were spoken (channeled) to me through my spirit guide Lizzy. I do not wish to lose what it is she has expressed to me. My greatest wish is that you receive it, just as I have received it. With Love, with Trust, with Humility.*

***Kathleen Garbe-Modzelewski***

Garbe's Collection
P O Box 26124
Frascr, MI 48026-6124
Toll Free # 1-877-860-2100 code #192101
e-mail: Garbescollec@acninc.net

# Chapter one

## A NEW BEGINNING

Message from Lizzy:

This book is going to be one of greatness, of love, and tranquility. It will mean something to all that pick it up into their hands and who look upon it with their eyes and who hear about it with their ears. This book will contain something for all. Meaning for all. No matter how small, it shall be a beginning. A small step in a big way. A door shall open and this will make room for someone else to give and to receive. A beginning. A new start.

For this is what a Butterfly Within shall be. Not what it shall be, but what it is. We all live in a cocoon of some sort. Whether its good or bad is of no concern now. What is of concern is the nature of a new beginning. We put this wall up around us and bury ourselves in the worries of others, problems, concerns, and the problems of the world. New and old beliefs of others – half-truths – we bury ourselves so deep it feels as if we are suffocating. We are in hiding and when we come out, we want what every one of us wants. We want a new start, a new beginning. We want the worries to be gone. The problems to be gone. The lies to be gone. We want to stop hiding. We want to come out of our cocoon a new person. One in which we can be free. One of beauty, freshness, and wholeness. One in which you can breathe in and out and not get terrified of this world of ours. We want beauty back, love back, freedom back, and peace back in our lives. We are tired of the hectic, maddening, mumble jumble of our world. The fighting, crimes, and uncertainty. We want our children to grow up in a clean, loving society. We want to share and care for them. We want to join them in the future. We want our grandchildren to know us, share with us, and be with us. We want what everyone wants, craves, and dreams of. We want a new beginning of beauty, prosperity and love. We want to be that butterfly. As we watch, we see that the caterpillar crawls along the ground, the trees, and the leaves scooting along waiting to get stepped on. Then he climbs into a cocoon and surrounds himself with protection and then after a certain amount of time, he decides to come out again and to give it another try. This time he comes out with beauty, freedom to fly here, there and wherever his heart takes him. He has learned the hard way. All grown up and starting again. We all can do this. We all can give of ourselves – to ourselves, the gift that screams of joy and beauty. That gift is to love ourselves. For only then can and will we be able to love others unconditionally. We will be free. As free as the butterfly and as beautiful as the butterfly. For we shall become whole once again. To give of ourselves to those that seek our wisdom and our love. What a gift. What a beautiful gift you can bestow upon yourself. The gift of the butterfly.

Dear Friends

I come to you to share my experience of my coming out. I was once the caterpillar crawling around not knowing what it was I wanted out of life, but knowing I was not getting it. The confusion, sickness, heartache. Most of us have been there. Lots of us are going there and yet some are there as we speak. We live in a world of hardness, grayness, selfishness and madness. I could go on. There is no use. We all know since we live in this world. But do you know there is another world. One of beauty, calmness, sharing, laughing, giving and loving. This world is here among all of us. You have to dig a little deeper to find it. When you find it, oh, when you find it, you will never, never, want to let go of it. For the feeling that comes with this world is one of greatness, wholeness, and unconditional love. When you acquire this love, you want to do something absolutely crazy with it. You want to give it to another and another and yet another. You want to share it. You want to give of the gift you have received. For in this way, you know that each time someone is looking for this world, it will be that much easier for him or her to find it. If we give of our gift, then we open them up and there is more for the next person that comes looking for our beautiful world. Then, what of the other world? Well, here is the craziest thing of all. If we have this world of giving, of sharing, laughter, wholeness and loving, why would we need this other world which is so sad and desperately miserable? The answer is so very simple. We would not! We could and we should all put a hand in this mixture of goodness. Let's get rid of the unwanted hatred, drugs, killings, and by God, bring the light in. The goodness, the sunshine, the laughter and the want of beauty, trust, sharing, and most of all, the want of loving. Love your neighbor as you love yourself. First, just learn to love yourself and then we can begin to rebuild this beautiful loving world we call our home.

Yes, child, we feel within our hearts and our souls. No different than you. Yet there is a difference, for we have love for all and do not judge anyone. Who are we to criticize anyone? We do not walk in his shoes. We shall only love him and hope that love is enough to bring him around to learn to love himself. For this is where it all begins. There is a beginning and hopefully, there will never be an end. Amen.

# Chapter two

## THE COMING OUT

We wrap ourselves in this protective cocoon. We stay – we hide. But are we hiding? Are we changing? You see, while we are in our protective place, many things happen to us in our lifetimes and as these things happen, we slowly break loose of this cocoon. When we find ourselves on the inside looking out, the world to us is a scary place.

When you place yourself in a cocoon, it is for protcction. This world can be rough. While there, we see our lives like an old movie running very slow. We see all. Where we have been, where we are now, and what we want in our future. We wonder, we ask, can we change? Will

God let us change? Will our friends accept our change? And most of all, can I change? The answer is simple. Most answers are: people do not accept the answers sometimes, because they are so simple. It does not have to be difficult. The answer is yes. Now, the difficulty comes. Changing! Working toward the change! Making the change and accepting the change. It does not matter what others feel. It is your change and yours alone. Will it affect them? Of course, it will. How could goodness not affect the next person? Whom will it affect the most? You! You and you alone are the most important at this time. Will God let us change? God will be holding your hand and walking beside you with an encouraging smile on His face. Yes, changes are possible. Some big, some small. It does not matter. What does matter is that the change is good, loving, and nurtures your very soul. You can breathe in with the light of forgiveness and breathe out with the light of love. As you change ever so slowly, you see that new world we have spoken of. As you catch a glimpse of this new world, you will want more. It is a high that is like no other. You do not need alcohol, drugs, or any man-made product for this high. This high is FREE! A little work on your part is all that is required. So, can we change? The answer is YES, we can. Now, a question to you. Will you change?

We are waiting for your answer. Only you know what that is.

# Chapter three

## YOU DO NOT WALK ALONE

We come to you to share with you that you are not alone. We know many times in your lives, you feel like you are fighting the whole world alone. Everything in every way is going bad. One thing after another falling in around you. One more thing and you feel that you will scream. How can all of this be happening to you? It could not get any worse. What can happen next? Do these words sound familiar to you? We hear them all the time. Let us be the first to tell you. It could be worse. Much worse. How lucky and fortunate you are to only have had that happen to you. My child, there is always a worse side to everything. When something bad happens, do this. Think to yourself how lucky and fortunate that we are here helping you. To stop whatever it was. Heal whatever it is. To thank God for the outcome. It could have been much worse. There is a good side to everything. I know sometimes we search, we wonder, and still we do not understand why this has happened to us. Let me say this. As you go on with your life, you will look back and you will see and then you will understand why it happened as it did. If it did not, you would not have developed as you are doing now. Things happen for change, development, and for reasons yet to be discovered. Change is growth. Remember this, when you feel you cannot possibly take another problem, call on us. We walk beside you. We are here to help you. We help, whether or not you ask. When you do ask, we are right there beside you. Our hands are out. Our hearts are open. We take as much of the load as possible. That's why you always make it. God never gives you more than you can handle, especially when his helpers are around.

God bless you, child.

You know, Lizzy, when I get where I feel I can no longer take anymore, I gather all my problems and put them into God's hands. I actually see his large and loving hands in front of me as I speak these words to him. "God, I can no longer handle these problems. I'm putting them into your hands knowing you will handle them all. I thank you, God." I feel better. Like I have just erased some terrible pressure off my chest. Knowing that God will handle it for me. This has worked wonders in my life and has helped so much to lessen all my worries.

Child, you could not have said it any better. God is here for every child and adult alike. He treats everyone with love and kindness. What He would do for you, He would do for the next. His hands are big and there is a lot of room for more to reach out to Him. They only need let Him into their lives.

Yes, I believe you are right. You know I always believed in God, His angels, and His helpers. I just always thought I had to be perfect to get His love. Oh, don't get me wrong. I used to pray very hard. In fact, I used to say my prayers at night and fall asleep only to awake with my hands still together to continue my prayers till I was finished. Oh, yes, I believe in prayer. I believed you should not use God's name in vain, or He would punish us. Do not lie, for He would punish us. Our punishment in Church was prayers and then we were all better until the next time. There was always a next time. For as you grow up, from a child's view, fibs, and name-calling was and always will be wrong. Why would anyone tell a child that God would punish him or her? God is all-good. God does not punish. Were prayers a punishment? (five Hail Mary's and ten Our Fathers) No!

Punishment it was not, but we sure learned how to pray. So as you see, God does not punish. God only loves. Sometimes the lessons that come our way are hard. With

God's help, we can get through anything. Going back to my childhood, we dreaded going to church and sitting for 45 minutes and learning what? Our rear ends were sore from the hard benches. We didn't understand Latin. When they changed to English, it was worse. We still did not understand it, but at least in Latin, it sounded so beautiful. There were so many rules. We wore doilies on our heads if we were female. Why just the girls, I wondered. Yet, I knew I could not walk in until something was on my head. I didn't want to walk in anyway. I knew I must for my parents had sent me. Were they with me? NO! Why, I wondered. My brother and I would walk to church and as we got closer, my brother would tell me where he would meet me when church was over (he skipped). I could not do that for I knew I could not look my mother in the eye and tell her I was there if I was not. I needed to go, for I could not tell a lie. I always wondered why my brother could and he became quite good at it, and I could not. I just thanked God that my parents never asked me if my brother was sitting next to me. Then, I would have been caught. God does work in mysterious ways. Thank you God, for the understanding of a little girl.

Now, as I am grown and I look back on my childhood religion and beliefs, I know that every family does its best with what it has to work with. I do not regret those days. I now take pleasure in the big beautiful churches where God speaks of his love to all that listen.

Now, I see with my inner eye, my heart, and my soul. I know churches are wonderful, for they bring masses of people together to spread the word of God of love and of light. As adults, we can pick our own church as our home. The place that sings in our hearts of goodness and love. What I want to express to all of you is this. Please do not use our God- yours and mine – for punishment. For he does not and will never do this. He is a God of goodness, pureness and lovingness. He reaches out to each and every one of us with his love. He touches our hearts and our souls with goodness. I ask that you see the light – the white light of protection that surrounds each and every one of us. How can a God so loving be anything but good? God loves you as he has always loved you. Take this word and share it with another. The word I give to you my friend, is LOVE. Use it well. God speed.

# Chapter four

## DEATH AND BEYOND

Good morning, child, and a blessed one at that. The sun shines, the wind blows, the birds sing. Let the sunshine in child, it will awaken your soul and bring to life all that we need.

Thank you Lizzy, I shall.

Child, many people wonder about many things, but are afraid to ask. If we could take a poll and ask them of their worries, or wonders, what do you think they would ask of us?

I think one of the questions would be about death. Where do we go? What do we do? What happens to us? For there is much wasted worry on this.

Yes, child, this is one of our biggest questions. We see it everyday. With so much happening and death all around, you tend to keep this buried inside of yourself with a fear of death knocking at your door. Let me say this to you, child. We need for all to lessen their worries for it does no good. When their time comes and messengers are sent to collect their loved ones and help them to come home once again, they are in their glory. There is no pain, worry, or fright. There is only freedom and excitement at seeing loved ones once again and peacefulness all at once. It is a coming home. The ones who tend to suffer are the ones that are left behind. Their loved ones are gone. They are now alone and frightened and they miss them, oh so badly. Yes child, these poor souls miss their loved ones. With time and love, they manage to go on – on their own. What we want to share with you is that you can help each other. Your loved one still sees you, hears you, and still wants to be with you. Yet he is torn for he has finally come home and also wants to be there. What you need to know child is that he is still very much alive. Not in the sense you know, you feel, or you see. Nevertheless, very much alive. He needs to rest, develop and continue on with his growth just as you do here while still on the earth plane. You need to focus on the good here. At this time in your life, you do not see the good. We shall point it out to you. Picture your loved one at their time of passing, lying in a bed, sick and suffering and just tired. Into their room, come those that have already made their transition. They stand at the end of the bed and smile at your loved one and say it is time now to come home. They have come to help them find their way home. They are now on a new journey of wisdom, pureness, and simplicity. They must learn all they can to heighten their ability to become enlightened with the knowledge they need for their life there. Now on this side, you sit next to your loved one and grieve with sadness for their passing. Your heart is broken and you just don't know how you could even live life without them. How can you go on? We shall tell you how. You need to think in the ways of our God. He is doing what He knows is right. Your loved one is not dead. He is very much alive. Not in the sense you know it, but here is the best part. You can learn how to communicate with them. You can feel closer than you ever thought possible. Different, yes; possible, yes; beautiful, yes. No one was taken from you. They were just given another life. One which they chose before they ever entered this lifetime. They came to you with love, they left you with love, and yet they give you love. My dear child, think in this way. Speak and he shall hear you. Listen and he shall reply. Whether it be a word, a thought, feeling, or sign. He has answered. Life continues in this way as we connect one by one. Grief lessens, love expands, growth becomes. This is the circle of life, death and oneness. The belief in yourself and the courage to go on. Whether you are the one making the transition, or the one staying behind. You are both making a new beginning, yet continuing on with the old.

Child, there are many ways to look at death. We ask you to think of us as your friends, protectors and navigators. Have no fear or worry, as we are always near.

Lizzy, that was a hard lesson. Yet you make it sound so easy.

Yes, Child, I guess we do. The reason being we celebrate here on this side when someone comes home. We welcome them with open arms and all loved ones join and the power of love takes over. You will understand this more when you join us at your time of transition.

Yes, I suppose I will. But, now I see the hurt and heartache on our side. We know this child and feel for all that lose their loved ones. The only thing we can say to you to help the pain is this. They are not suffering nor in pain. They are free to come and go. They hear you, love you, and will always watch out for you. Call on them when you need them and most of all. They are not **DEAD**. Death is such a final word. They are living much like you are but just somewhere else. In a place of beauty, love and tranquility. They will be there waiting for you when it is your turn to pass over. They have just gone before you, to check it out first. They will be there waiting with their arms open. With these few words, we hope we have eased some of your fears and worries. Love to all on your side and ours.

# Chapter five

## THE WORD

Good morning, Lizzy! Child, why is it that so many are afraid to say the word? What word is that, Lizzy? God! They are not afraid to say, Satan, Devil, witches, evil, maddening, scary, frightening. Now, those are words I would be afraid to say. Why the mix-up here?

We were always taught not to use God's name in vain. Also, nobody wanted to be known as a church person. Everytime you meet someone, God this, God that, and God, God, God. They chase you away. We call this bible thumping. Preaching, screaming, and it just pushes people away. When you look at these people, a lot of them are frauds. Using God's name to lie and steal from the one's that believe. They use people. Not all, mind you.

But the word is not good out there. They are using Him and His name for their own good, and their own selfishness. That is why we have all taken God into our hearts and pray silently. So many have stopped going to churches for the want of peacefulness. So many churches tell people how much they have to donate in order to attend their domain. All this does is push people out and back into their homes not to attend and to take their prayers home with them. Do these people believe in our father's work? Yes, with all their hearts. Do they want to be close to Him? Yes, with all of their hearts! Do they believe in him and his love? Yes, they do with all their hearts. Then why cannot these simple folks come out of their closets, homes and rebound in the joy and harmony and blessedness of our father? Why must they stay hidden away to pray while all of these others are out there yelling and screaming of God's love? Let them join their hands and rejoice in his love. For as soon as this happens the users will be thrown to the side and they will not be able to use the name of God. They will no longer have the power, for the true believers will know the difference for they will feel it inside of their soul.

Child, do not ever be afraid to use God's name. The use of his name said in pureness can only bring love and tranquility into your life, your heart, and your whole being. Feel him and his presence and share him with all that listen. Share him with all that listen but share him in a way that does not turn a head or a heart away. For everyone out there is looking for him in their own way. Some more than others and others not even aware of their search. Nevertheless, their soul is crying and awakening and wants to be heard. Use God's name in healings and in love. In teachings and in harmony. In pureness and in vitality. Only God can give this to all. All who ask and all who do not. He gives it out. The only problem he finds is that not everyone is taking it. He can give but you must be willing to receive. This is a gift. From him to us. Open your hearts, your souls, and let the sun shine in. For you are aware that everywhere you look, see, touch and breathe, God has made for us. So you do see. Even if you are not aware of it, you are receiving gifts from our father.

# Chapter Six

## BELIEVE IN THE POWER AND LET THE HEALING BEGIN

Lizzy, going back a few years, I liked to go to different churches and see what they all did. How they attended their churches, the beliefs, practices. I must say many of us I'm sure have attended different churches, growing up. Some of these churches scared me. Some were beautiful, some charming, some happy. The one that stands out in my mind is the one that I went to visit a friend. I walked in and heard all this yelling, screaming, crying, banging, and what I thought to be fighting. I asked my friend what was happening and was informed that they were just praying. How can this be? Praying, not fighting. How can you take the name of our Father and turn it into a screaming, yelling fit? I do not know. For God is peace, love, and tranquility. Somewhere along the lines we got our God's mixed up. I thanked them, left, but never forgot. Do I judge? No. Not at this time. Then, yes I did. Did I have a right? No. If it works for them, then it's right. Does it work for me? No. For I am not a violent or loud person. I need calmness in my life. If I want to wrestle, I'll find one of my children or grandchildren to play with. Now I can look back and smile and understand. Then I just ran. For fright drove me away. Experiences, yes, we have all had them. I would like to share just one more short story with you.

My daughter and I took a trip to the warm state of Florida to visit family and friends. While there, we attended this small church. I had many problems I was trying to solve and many hurts that I was trying to mend. Church to me sounded like a wonderful idea. We went with a friend. My first impression, small. My second impression, different. My third impression, ask God for his help and just flow with the service. Now I really cannot even remember the service, but what I can remember is the way I felt. That was not my church and I did not believe in their beliefs but I did believe in God. When we need something in our lives changed, we so desperately pray to God to help us, do we not? So this is what I did. People were lining up for a healing. I figured it couldn't hurt. I stood in line. A healing, what's that? What would they do to me? Well, I got all the answers I needed about two minutes later. They stood in front of me and asked me what I wanted and what I needed most in my life, and I answered peace. They touched my head, prayed for me and God to send this peace into my life. I must say if it had ended there it would have been fine. The most unusual thing happened. I started to shake, cry and an uncontrollable gift came into my life that day. The gift of belief. That God works in mysterious ways. I can actually say I was healed. At least I was on my way to being healed. The rest was up to me. He gave me what it was I needed. He gave me a sign, a belief, and a knowing that God hears all and is with all that ask. My daughter witnessed this and was as shook up as I was. That evening, someone else said he would like to give me a healing the following day and now I'm going to go back to that bible thumping person. Well, this was one of them. I looked at my daughter and said, "pack your bags – we're out of here." For I knew then that I would never let a non-believer do a healing on me. After what had just happened to me, no one and I mean no one can top that. Yes, God does work in mysterious ways. I must point out to you, that was my first and only healing in a church or any other place for that matter. I knew it was real. I knew it was powerful and I also knew it would never happen again.

Now as I look back, I do not regret the experience. What a blessing. I do not regret not letting the other fellow compete and try his healing on me. What I do regret is not knowing the difference. It took me many years to figure it out. I wanted nothing to do with healings, for this fellow turned me off. For I knew he was just using it for his own glory and justification. Now, 15 years later, a healer myself (yes, you heard me), I had the pleasure of meeting a wonderful teacher. I remember the first time he said healing. You want what! Me to heal someone? No way. He was insistent. He explained, "no, dear child, you are not doing the healing. You are just the instrument in which to be used. God does the healing." Put that way, okay. I'll give it a try. At first, the feeling was I felt foolish. Then when I went into prayer and asked God for his strength and power of healing and let him know that I was available for his services to be used through me if he wished. I had this overwhelming beautiful feeling of oneness. Connected to him to help others. Through his good graces and lovingness, how can a healing be bad? It can't. All it takes is the belief in God and his strength to heal all that ask. For it shall be his will to give of himself to you his child. So I say to you, believe in the power and let the healing begin.

# Chapter seven

## BELIEVE IN YOURSELF

To believe in someone or something is so very important. We all must believe in ourselves in order to grow. The belief in yourself is the one thing all must have. For without belief, what would there be? All need a direction in life. From birth on you are instilled with all kinds of beliefs. Some good, some bad, and some we just don't have any idea of what to do with. But these beliefs come from someone else. These are not your beliefs. Your mother, father, sister, or maybe it was your brother. A cousin, or maybe even a friend. Put all these ideas in your head. Your mind is filling with wants, dislikes, hearsay, do's and don'ts, yes's and no's. What you should like and not like. Who you should speak to and not speak to. Listen and not listen to. How to be, act, and even how to dress. Everyone has a special code of ethics. Do we need to follow these rules when deep down we know they do injustice to someone else? Do we need to follow advice when we know the harm it could bring to another? Whether it is physical or mental? A hurt is a hurt by any means. Do we have a right to say and do injustice because someone else instilled this belief in us from the time of birth? The answer to this is one in which we all know. But many are afraid to go against the grain. To stand up for their beliefs. For the knowing of what's right and wrong. You are no longer children. You no longer have to do what you are told. If it is wrong, change. If it is right, do it. If it is unknown, work it out for yourself. For you and only you know of the goodness in which you would like to receive something. Why not use yourself as the vantagepoint? If you would like it, would they not? If it pleased you, would it not please them? If it harmed you, would it not do the same to someone else? If it displeased you, would it not also displease another? Use yourself as the object. Do unto others, as you would wish them to do unto you. As grown adults, you can no longer put the blame elsewhere. For you are the true holder of all as you enter adulthood. You cannot be pushed, shoved, or told what to do. For you must make your own mind up and come to some kind of conclusion on the why and why nots; how and how nots; truths and lies that are given to everyone of you from the time of birth. Complicated you ask. Yes, sometimes it can be. For everything is not black and white. Sometimes it is very colorful to make you believe in the unbelievable. Yes, you have to search deep inside yourself to know the answer. Each and every one of us has the wisdom and the insight to know good from evil and love from hate. Go within my child. Go within for the answers are all there. Waiting for you. Go through all the jumbled up mess and straighten it out. Throw the bad away. Never to return and help the good to go on forever. In this way you shall succeed in whatever it is you have your sights set on. Your heart and your beliefs are yours alone. Go within Child and start cleaning out your cobwebs.

I shall, as I know everyone feels like this at one time or another. I remember that as a child I wanted to help everyone. There was this girl in my class. Everyone was mean to her. She was dirty and she had an unclean smell to her. Her long hair was in knots and never brushed. I always felt bad when other kids teased her. (Still to this day, I do not understand how children can be so cruel.) Never would I have said anything to intentionally hurt someone. I am not saying I never hurt someone. For with my quick and foolish mouth, things have darted out without mindful thoughts behind them. What I am saying is never would I intentionally say hurtful things to others to make them cry or hurt in anyway. But there are those who do not think in these ways and to make themselves feel like a bigger person, they become the bosses and the others, the followers, and then you have the losers. The ones, that people pick on. She's in tears; the bully is picking on her, others laughing and I'm angry. As a child, I was taught not to look down on others for there are always people worse off than ourselves. To count our blessings. We did not have much in ways of the rich, but what we did have was love, warmth, food and clothing. Enough to get us by. Enough to know someone cared. As a child you know no difference if you do not have it or live near it. As you grow up, you soon learn all about it for it is thrown in your face everyday. The want of more. But yet, even back then I would still give to this little girl my friendship. I had more than she had. I had love from within which I shared with my newfound friend. Was it hard? Yes. Did my old friends tease me? Yes. Give me a hard time? Yes, to all of the above. Was it worth it? Yes, it was. For even to this day, I remember her well. For you see, when she washed her face, put on clean clothes and combed her hair, she was just like the rest of us. Then the teasing stopped. She was forgotten and they looked for their next target. I wondered, were there others like me. Always trying to help the underdog. I guess there had to

be. God would not have put only one little girl in a low-income family to do his mending. I'm sure there are others like me, and someday when I grow up, I just know God will introduce me to all the others I missed so much growing up without. As an adult, I look back at my life in different terms of endearment. For the love within me came out. Who taught me, who helped me and who was there to get me through all those tough times? There is only one answer
to that.

> Thank you God, from my child's heart to your heart. From my adult heart to all hearts. For I have learned my lesson well.

P.S. I wish to thank you for finally letting me meet all those other kids that were just like me. Now that we are adults, we know where to go to find our friends. The true believers in love and kindness. Our wish is to find more and more of the same kind. Come join in our journey and like-minded people will always surface and gather in God's home. Our garden of pleasure is yours for the picking. Our love to you. From a child's heart to your heart. Love to all that come and venture in a garden which shall become their garden as well.

# Chapter eight

## A GIFT

This is what we are. A gift to each and everyone that we touch and which touches us. A gift that we wish to open. We are all wrapped up in beautiful paper and ribbon galore. The outside is so beautiful that you do not want to open it. You are almost afraid to open it. Whatever lies inside cannot possibly be as nice as the outside package.

Or can it? You can and you should, because beauty lies within. The beauty within should outshine the outside of the package for it is only a cover up. What is real lies inside.

Something you can touch, be, see, feel, for this is

what shines within. The love of the gift. Whichever gift it is you wish to give. The greatest gift anyone could ever give would be the gift of himself or herself – to you, their friend. To touch, be, see, and know the difference. This gift which you give so generously is the gift of love, belief, freedom, and choice.

Lizzy, you always seem to be able to hit home with whatever it is you speak on.

You know everyone of us wants the perfect body, shape, beauty and to be wanted, sought after, and to be popular. As a child you can sit back and wish, not knowing how to go about it. Jealous of the girls and boys who are popular and wondering why it's not you. Later, as you grow, you start to understand that it's not all on the outside. What lies within is what matters. This is so very true. It's more than that. You have to feel good about yourself and help yourself to do better. You may never become that gorgeous blond, skinny body, and built like a centerfold that all guys drool over. You can look nice, clean, and attractive. You need to feel good about yourself in order to feel good about anything else in this world of ours.

Sometimes we are our own worst enemy when we could become our best friends. This is where we need to go within and see what it is we really want. Do we want to smile when we look into that mirror or do we want to be disgusted? Do we want to feel good about ourselves when we go out or do we want to hide? Do we want people to take notice of us and to see us as we are inside and out? We must present ourselves as a beautiful gift in order for others to feel comfortable. We must want to open the gift that stands in front of us. In doing so, you are not only helping others, but you are also helping yourself to be that person that you want to be. The gift you have just received is one of specialness. Love for you, from you to them. The gift you ask. Who is it for? Why don't you open it and see!

The gift from me to you.

God speed.

# Chapter nine

## THE BIG PICTURE

Now you see the big picture. Never limit yourself to only one idea. Open yourself up for there is a whole world out there just waiting for you. One you never even thought of before. A new door opening just waiting for you to walk through. A new experience, a new beginning, never to end. What a joyride you are on, the best part of it is, that every single person can be on this joyride along with you. If not with you, along side you on one of their very own. What a beautiful thought. For that is exactly where it starts. A beautiful thought that expands into a beautiful being, a thing, a journey. For you are never alone. There will always be those you take along on your way. Whether it be a journey for one, two or more, will always be touched along the way. For that is how it works. The one thing we must realize is that this journey is one of love, of knowledge, for many will welcome this touch. A journey of displeasure, hurt and pain would not be welcome by others. Nevertheless, they would be touched. This is why you and you alone must decide what journey you will be taking. As the saying goes, the high road or the low road. The decision is yours. Think it over carefully. For what you decide, you also decide for the next person along the way. The one you touch and the one they touch. It is a chain reaction. It can be a high or a low, good or bad, prison or freedom, emptiness or wholeness. The decision is yours child. Make this one count.

You know that as a child you see many things. Experience many things and do many things that we are not proud of. As adults. We look back. Now, we wonder how could we have done that, said that, let it happen. We did it for that reason. We were children, young adults. We learn unfortunately through our mistakes. The hard way. We all have that secret that lies within us. The regret of something unfinished, uncompleted. The want of forgiveness. This can be done. By one and only one person. As an adult, forgive yourself. Forgive the child in you so many years ago. Let it go. Stop torturing yourself and let it go. Forgiveness starts at home, in your temple. Then and only then can you continue on. Do not let it eat at you. For the gnawing never stops. Just keeps festering and festering till your one big hurt. Let the hurt go and underneath all the hurt you will still find that little child cowering. Let him or her be free to stand up tall and be heard. To become the adult he or she wishes to be. Not to be ashamed for it was not our fault or the fault of others. They knew no better. Hug yourself inside and out and be free to love yourself; all of yourself. For the child within you waits.

That touched my heart. It made me think of my childhood at one of my most traumatic times in my life. One I never shared with anyone till recently. For it was my secret. I tortured myself, felt embarrassed, and just wanted to hide. Why me? Why was this happening to me? As you said, I was a child with a problem. I wet the bed. I still to this day have a problem admitting what I used to do. Like I was the only one in the whole world that it ever happened to. Ashamed, mortified, embarrassed, and scared. Those are the words I remember. I think and I feel when even I think of it. I'd rather not think and tell the whole world about such a thing. Instead of being proud of myself when I no longer did it. No, that's not the case. The case being I'm still embarrassed. Still ashamed. Still feel like the terrible little girl that I thought I was. Why you ask? For what was done to me. Yes, I wet the bed. Yes, I was embarrassed and ashamed and yes, I wanted to hide myself away never to return. I could not stop wetting the bed. I was afraid to fall asleep at night for fear of a wet bed when I woke in the morning. I would get in trouble from my parents. I remember being yelled at. Why was I doing it? Why did I not wake up and go to the bathroom. Why was I so lazy? That was a good question which I asked myself over and over again. Why, why, why. I tried to stay awake and after awhile I found it easier to sleep on the floor, for then they would not find the bed wet. I felt no escape. No one to help me in my dilemma. I cried myself to sleep. Why was I such a bad girl? What did I do wrong to deserve such a thing? It got to where I could not even spend the night at my girlfriends for accidents continued on for quite a few years. As I got older, I got angrier. Well, God sent me an answer to my prayers. He sent my grandfather to me. Weekends during the summer were spent at my grandparents' cottage on the lake. My world of paradise and happiness and the love of my grandparents taught me much. My grandfather took it upon himself to wake me every night, at least once a night, to go to the bathroom. They put a plastic sheet on top of the mattress so I would not ruin the mattress, which took my guilt away, and the fear. On the days I still had an accident, I went to the laundry mat with Gramps to help him wash clothes and then came home and hung them on the line. I felt whole once again. The days of success were greeted with approval and smiles. The days of accidents were quoted with, "its okay. Today's another day." They did it in such a way that as a child I only knew I felt good inside about myself again. For now, I had help and someone to teach me and not yell at me and make me feel ugly inside. As I look back now as an adult I know it was not my parents' intention to hurt me in any way. My mother was an only child and apparently never had my problem, and my father came from a very strict family where I'm sure none had this problem. I was the oldest daughter with a problem that neither knew how to handle. They did the best they knew. With love for us all. As an adult, I soon found out why I had this problem as a child. My daughter also had this problem. It is a medical problem. I took her to the doctor and through treatment we were able to control this. What kind of treatment you wonder. The same my grandfather gave to me. A system, training to wake yourself up every night, and not to sleep so sound. The nights when I took the stairs up to awaken my daughter I said thanks Gramps for being there when I needed you. From a girl's heart to her Gramp's heart. Have faith; love shall win.

Now that I have shared my story with you, I have removed one of the biggest burdens of my childhood. For there is no longer any shame. For myself and surely never was for my daughter and hopefully I never instilled this in my daughter. For life gives us many twists in our journey. Many lessons. Learn them well and carry them on. For they are grand. From your hand to the next.

Thank you Lizzy for letting me share that story. That was very difficult for me. I was always embarrassed and hurt by it. Now, I feel relieved for I knew I had to experience it in order to help my daughter when she developed the same problem. The one thing I must say is that I also felt the frustration that my parents must have felt for me. For I felt it, yet I knew how my daughter felt also. For many times I would go up to awaken her and she would be up and changing her bed. So I would make the trip up those stairs earlier next time. We would conquer this, we would win, for we were in this battle together.

Love from a mother to her daughter.

A special place there will always be for my grandfather meant so much to me. He was there in times of worry and fret. He made me forget all my hurts and regrets. He brought out the sun to shine in my eyes and let my heart sing from morning till night.

I love you Gramps!

# Chapter ten

## MOTHER EARTH

"Good morning, Child." "What a beautiful morning". "I stood and I listened to your prayers." " Many were for others, some for you and for all children and adults alike." "I should have put Mother Earth in there and also our planet."

"Yes, Child, you should always add those two to your prayers." The reason being Mother Earth, our planet, and our world need your help and not only your help but all must help. We all must pray for the white light of our father to sweep this world through and let the light shine through for all to achieve and for the Earth to continue in a much better way. For much destruction comes its way. Everything from garbage, to poisons is infecting our Planet Earth. One which used to be clean is now one of uncleanness. One of impurity, destruction, and one with war. Not only war in terms of fighting and killing, but also war with each other. Likes, dislikes, lies, yelling, swearing, hitting, stealing, promises not, kept, uncaring, undoing, unpleasantness. Should I go on? No, I should not for we all know of this. All participants in this to some degree. Do we not agree that this must STOP? Before we destroy the very thing that means so much to all of us. Our planet! Mother Earth has been good to us has she not? Do you not breathe in her air, drink of her water, eat of her food? Then how can you be so cruel to someone that has done nothing but give of herself to you? How can you be so blind as not to see what you are doing? So selfish as not to care of the outcome? Well, here is a little bulletin. It is time to start caring. You can no longer look away and let the next person do it. You can no longer ignore the warning signs. You can no longer blind yourself to the wrong doings of our Planet Earth. We live here, we use her, and she is good to us. Is it not time that we reverse the process and start giving back to what we take for granted every day? For one day you shall awaken to what you have done. When you reach for that water and find it not drinkable, when you reach for that food and find it not edible, or take that breath of fresh air to find yourself choking and coughing for it is unbreathable. What shall you do then? What will happen to all of you then? What will become of your planet then? Oh, the planet will still be here, but will you? This I ask of you. Think real hard on all that you do. For everyone needs to do his share. Become one. Not only with each other, but one with our Mother Earth. For it takes both of you to produce what it is you need for your life. Now, is it not time that you did your share? For Mother Earth has surely done hers! I leave this with you Child. Remember. Think real hard on this one for it is a mighty big one. Without her, you have nothing and we mean nothing.

Love to you all who read of our words and to all those that do not!

Thank you Lizzy and love also to you.

Lizzy, as a child you see many things, experience many things and do many things that are big no-no's as a child soon learns. For instance, cleaning paintbrushes and putting them into cans of gasoline or paint thinner to soak, and then dumping this out in the yard. Now, I think of the poor Earth as it cried out. Throwing plastic wrappers into the water. Now, I think of the poor fish as they choked to death on someone's litter. Let alone polluting our waters.

Garbage being dumped on the streets instead of cans or bags. Now, I see how all the bugs and rats came about. We are feeding the unwanted. To kill the bugs and rats, we have to use poisons which also kill us. So I ask of all, who is killing whom? Take a real long hard look at yourself. You are no longer children. You are now adults with an understanding of an adult. From one adult to another, let us teach our children how to respect our Mother Earth. For we may no longer be here but our children will be and their children. Do we want to watch our children and grandchildren suffer and struggle for our mistakes. I think not. I know I surely do not want my children to suffer. How about you?

# Chapter eleven

## TO BELIEVE IN THE UNBELIEVABLE

Child, we are touched as always with your prayers. Our Father listens to you as he listens to all that call on him. His ears are always open as is his heart. Know he will do what must be done. It may not be as you have asked or what you expect. But nevertheless it shall be. In his pureness and goodness, your prayers will always be answered.

Thank you for your thoughts on this subject. It always makes me feel good to have validation of such things.

Yes, Child, we know this of you and of all. For you are no different then the rest. We all want validation, proof. So we make sure every now and then you receive such in order to remember you are not alone. For we walk beside you.

To know this helps extremely. To believe in the unbelievable. What a journey. You know, Lizzy, just a few years ago, people would look down on us for even talking aloud about such things. Now, it's becoming acceptable. Don't get me wrong. You still can't go somewhere and just start talking about my spirit guides, my angels, my teachers, meditation, healings, and so on. For there are some that would lock us up, even in this day. But what we can do is seek out the believers, meet with like-minded people, have classes that teach and help develop our senses, our vibrations, that we may become one, a wholeness. As we look around we slowly sees people speaking of angels. That's not a frightening thing to most any more. Nurses and students taking healings into the hospitals. What a giant step for mankind. Books and more books, being written on the subjects of souls, spirits, astral projections, psychics, trance, mediumship, channeling. Meditation is another that people are not afraid of, for it is much like yoga. A sort of prayer and yet an exercise. It's like we wait for the stamp of approval before it can be taken into our homes. What's happening now is people are becoming independent and are deciding for themselves that something is missing from their lives. There is more to this universe then the eye sees. We feel it all around us. It's called the awakening. For it's always been there. Just not taken seriously. People have always gone to psychics. It started out as fun, a game, and a treat, amusement. Then turned into want for they found the words to be truthful and meaningful. People want answers now to questions they have always had but were afraid to ask. Death was a big one, scary one. But one not spoken of. Now it's being shouted to the world. We do not die! What a wonder. What a belief. But can we believe. For I believe this is where it all starts. The knowing that we do continue on. The knowing that our soul will continue to grow. Knowing that death does not await us. Where does that leave the fear? I shall tell you where that leaves the fear. Nowhere. For it is gone once we learn of the beauty that awaits us. That is why this journey is being taken by more and more people everyday. For the fear is gone. If there is no fear, then no harm can come to them that pass over. Golly, we have to learn all about this wonderful world before we leave so we are ready. Do you not want to be ready and waiting when your time of transition comes? The best part of this all is the power of learning. That's why we have our groups of circles, classes, books, healers, meditation, angel pictures, statues, and pins. Jesus is not alone in his journey. He has just been joined by a following of seekers. A new beginning, like-minded people join together and speak of the truths, the wants and the beliefs. We have put the trashing aside and opened up our hearts to each other and helping each other to grow. For with growth comes love to expand to the next, to listen, to teach, to heal to be whatever it is you wish to be. Yes, the word is spreading. It was the best-kept secret of all mankind. Now, the secret is out and is being used daily by those that want to grow. That want to be whatever it is they seek. For through these teachings, I have learned one thing. Jealousy does not exist. We learn all we can, we give all we can, we grow all we can and we are proud of each person that grows, and their accomplishments and their oneness. That is the difference between right and wrong. Selfishness and wanting. Directing and being directed. I feel that everyone of us is connected. If you succeed from a lesson I taught you, to go on and become a teacher of your own, I am proud. So very proud. For that is what we are supposed to do. We are supposed to give of our hearts, souls and our very beings. Not hold back. Give, learn all you can in the process for there will always be another teacher, another student. For not one knows all. That's why we have teachers, books, groups and variety. Choose who you pick wisely. Feel the vibration and the oneness of the class. But know this, not only one person can teach all. You need to reach out and experience. Bring it all together and make it whole. As in everything else. You have the bad with the good. So go with your heart and soul and feel. You will know the difference.

Child, as always you touch a subject that is so true. There are many teachers, some good and some bad. But as in everything you do, you must choose. Choose wisely. You see you need the goodness, truthfulness, the opening, and not the controlling. The want of helping and developing the student. Yet as you say, there are many good teachers and they all teach differently. All need variety to open. To learn, to become a teacher themselves. This journey is a long one. Never to finish till you cross over and even then it still continues on. For the more you develop the higher you go into the realms. What a beautiful concept. Do you not agree?

# Chapter twelve

## TRUST

Without trust, we have nothing. We must go within and we must trust not only the other, but we must also trust in ourselves. We must fill ourselves. We must fill ourselves with wisdom and belief and the knowing that all will be what it shall. We were put here on this earth plane to give of ourselves to ourselves. This includes trusting ourselves. For without this, we are only half of what we should be. The belief in ourselves, our world, our fellowman, is all of one belief, one trust. Our Lord put us here to be. What, you ask? Go within and ask this of yourself. Only you can answer this question. Only you know where it is you wish to be. Only you know how far you will go to accomplish this. Trust is worthiness in yourself, your partner, and your very being. If we cannot trust ourselves with our own life, then whom can we trust? Who can we follow? Who will answer our questions? How will we know the answers are trustworthy? This is why we need to go within. This is why we need to share. This is why we need to trust. If we are not trustworthy, then how can we reach out to Our Father for his love, for his understanding and for his wisdom? If we cannot give him this, in ourselves, then what can we give him?

Trust goes beyond the normal. Your job, your neighbor, your friend. We want to trust even that stranger on the street. But, can we? Should we?

Again, go within and ask. Should you trust a stranger? Will I be hurt? Harmed in any way? Will he laugh at me? Do I dare share something of the heart with my loved one? Can I trust them not to react in a bad way, or snicker at me? Again, I say to you. If you do not trust in your heart and yourself how can you trust in others?

Would a laugh be so harmful? Hurtful maybe, yet you could deal with it. For if you do not share, you cannot trust and if you cannot trust, you cannot learn. If you cannot learn, then you do not exist!

We must build our home in our heart, soul and our very being. To be able to trust, not only in yourself, but also in others, is Our Father's wish for all. What a beautiful, wonderful world we would live in then.

So what do you say? Do we trust? Or – do we not?

# Chapter thirteen

## THE ROSE TREE

Good morning to you, Child. As you look out into the day, do not see the gray as it appears out your window, but instead see the beauty that lies beyond the clouds, grayness, and wind. Somewhere behind those clouds you see there is a sun that is trying to get out. It must go through all of the other before it shines through. For you see we need the wind to dry up the water. The sun came out and melted the snow and now the sun goes away to let someone else come through to do its job. Do we care for it? Not really. Yes, we would want it sunny all the time if we could. Or would we? The sun can get very hot and very uncomfortable and then we wish for a cloud or two so we do not scorch. Do you see how we must use all we have to get where we want. We must travel unwanted territory in order to make our life complete. We must take on responsibilities, trials, and unwants in order to realize what it is we need in our lives. We must not only wish for the best for the best may not be what you think it is. For we must travel our path and work through our obstacles and barriers before we know what it is that we need. Even then, we may never know. Our life changes from day to day. We grow from a bud to a rose. From a single stem to a bush. From a bush to a tree. Then and only then shall we complete what it is that has been set before us? Yet even then to continue on like that tree for hundreds and hundreds of years. When we make our transition to the other side, we shall continue to blossom and what we have left behind as new buds on our tree (our children, friends and students) shall open up and develop yet another set of beautiful buds. A rose tree, you ask. Oh yes, I would like to be that rose tree that I see as clouds disperse and thin out, my oh my what do I see. Yes, I do see my rose tree. Now, of course, it's only a very small bush. But someday with work it shall stand tall among a whole orchard of rose trees. All smiling at the sun. Their faces will be tilted up and the smell of the rose could drift up to the skies and the sun will shine down. Together they shall become one. My question to you. Are you a rose in bloom?

Lizzy, as a child I was always afraid to pick flowers in a garden. They were too beautiful. I thought they would cry if I snipped them. I thought people would get mad. It was stingy to bring them inside for one to enjoy and not all outside. Since then, I have come a long way in my thinking on this. When you snip it, another blossoms in its place. The joy of having one of beauty inside to look at everyday and to go out and enjoy also. This is a beautiful realization. It's like your rose tree story. One is replaced by another and another. Also, the beauty, which lies inside, dries up whether we want it to or not. It must make this journey, but the bud is still there to carry on. Still, the same rose bush or tree as it grows and sheds the unwanted turning more beautiful and larger as time goes on. There is a certain amount of snipping, pruning, tending in order to become that beautiful tree. If you let it grow wild, it will still grow roses. What kind of roses? Not pretty one's; wild ones; smaller, snarly, and the beautiful bush has now become the garbled mess of prickly branches, thorns, and petals. Which would you want in your garden? This is what tending your garden means. Whether it is a rose bush or you. You need to tend it with kid gloves, piece by piece. In this way, we touch another and another and another and before you know what's happening, you have become that rosebush waiting and tending till you become the full fledged beautiful rosetree that awaits each and every one of us. I guess what I am saying is that I would much rather be the beautiful rose bush then the wild one. With a little work on my part and yours, I know we can accomplish this for I have faith in you my friend and also faith in myself. For I am a rose!

Yes, Child, that you are and one that is growing into a bush very quickly. Study hard, seek wisdom, know truth for what it is and by all means call on our God for guidance.

I shall. Thank you, Lizzy.

You are most welcome, Child.

# Chapter fourteen

## MEDITATION

Meditation is very special. It connects you with the inner-self the God self. It lets you reach where it is you long to be. The very core of your being. It helps you to center on yourself and others. This is the beginning. With this beginning, it continues to grow, and you continue to grow. You learn how to meditate and then when you need to connect, you go there instantly. You know how to travel to where it is you wish to be. Many answers await you there. Much wholeness, oneness, yet together with the entire universe. What used to be big is now very small, for you have made a connection. You now know the path. The route in which to go. This takes practice! It does not just come your way. You do have to work for it. If there were no work, you would not feel worthy of the greatness you have accomplished. We are not saying you have to sit for hours in meditation everyday. All it takes is a few times a week. A half-hour or so. Whatever is comfortable for you. Once in meditation it is so beautiful and time is not a concept. It just is. Sometimes you feel so wonderful, beautiful that you wish not to come back, but you must. The next experience will be one of such beauty also. Always to return to your world to turn around and return to ours. This meditative state is also your world. One in which you can reach when you need and also to learn from. Much truth lies within. This connection is one of greatness and holiness. One of total beauty. A oneness which each and every person should experience. Should connect to. For the beauty and wisdom lie waiting for you to make the next step.

Lizzy, you are so right.

Once I learned to meditate I started growing leaps and bounds. I used to think I didn't want to meditate because I don't have time for that. I tried and found something out. Something almost indescribable. Peacefulness, a wonder, world of beauty, colors, pictures, understanding. I learned how to go places, how to communicate with loved ones, how to connect with what was important to me. I found answers, strength, and wisdom. Almost like a class. I could ask a question and would receive an answer. The growth is unbelievable. Yet believable. I am experiencing it. If I were not, I would not believe what is happening to me. I am experiencing it and yet I still have to pinch myself to realize this is really happening to me. Me, a nobody! How can this be happening to me? The answer is easy. It's because it can happen to anyone and everyone who wishes to become closer to our world, the God world where Love, wisdom, tranquility, sharing, beauty, reign. What a beautiful world this is. Would you not want to step on board and give it a whirl?

Instruction. Find a quiet room. No ringing phones or voices. Playing low music tunes only, no words. (This is called meditation music). Light a white candle, and if you have incense, light it. If not, it's perfectly okay. The most important thing is quiet, low music, and a white candle. Now, go into prayer. This is what I do. Please feel free to say which ever prayer makes you feel the most comfortable. I myself sit down and say the Our Father," The Lords prayer." That prayer to me is one of the most powerful wonderful prayers ever written. I feel connected almost instantly. After the prayer, ask that you are surrounded by God's white light of protection. In this, I picture two hands (God's large hands) full of liquid light spilling down from his open hands over my head and surrounding my body to connect under my feet. It's as if I am in a bubble of white light. Now, I ask my spirit guides and teachers to come to me and to be with me to show me what it is they wish to show me. Take me somewhere beautiful and experience together. Once in meditation, you can ask almost anything and you will find the answers. If not this time, then the next or next. See yourself sitting in a beautiful garden or on the beach with the sun shining down on you. Use your imagination as a tool. Start out and then see where you go. You will go somewhere and experience something. Remember what it was. When you are ready, come back. Always thank your guides and teachers for they will be there for you the next time. Share this with someone or write it down and refer to it frequently. Your journey has just begun.

Yes, Child, their journey has just begun. We can make it even a little easier for them. Shall we try?

Yes, by all means!

Sit in quiet, music playing, white candle burning and welcome your loved ones, teachers, spirit guides and surround yourself with God's white light of protection. This is called meditative state (quiet). Now see yourself standing in a field looking all around. See the beautiful flowers. See that daisy looking up at you. Reach down and pick it, now smell it, feel it, how soft it feels. Now look straight in front of you at a path. Proceed down the path.

How good this feels and how beautiful. Now, you are winding a little and going down a short bank. Look! What is that? Do you not see it? Water. Hear it as it flows together. It looks like diamonds sparkling oh so brightly. Put your hands in and feel how cool it is. Now, bring some to your lips and taste of the freshness. That is what it is doing – refreshing you. Sprinkle some on your face and arms. Oh, how lovely. You are anxious as you see the path continues on and you would like to see where it leads you. Continue on when you are ready. Go around the water, or over the path. Whichever way you wish to go for it all connects at the same place. Once you are on the path, you see something sparkling ahead of you. What could it be? Pick it up. Look at it and place it in your pocket. Continue on. Now, we are going up hill. We are at the top of the hill looking down at a beautiful sight. See the butterflies playing in the flowers. Take your daisy and place it back where you got it. It is now whole once more. Thank the daisy for the beautiful walk. You are now home. Welcome Back.

Now questions to you:

1. What kind of flower did you see beside your daisy?
2. Walking the path, how did it curve and wind?
3. What kind of water did you see?
4. What path did you take, around or over?
5. What did you find shining on the path?

6. What color butterflies did you see?
7. What did you feel like on top of the hill
8. How did you feel once you put the Daisy back?

This is but a simple meditation of beauty and quest. You could take this walk several times and always see something different. As there is much to see. You shall find the peace within on your daily walks.

That was really beautiful. I'd like to take that walk.

Do Child. Go within and find the peace.

I shall.

# Chapter fifteen

## WHAT AM I GOING TO BE WHEN I GROW UP?

We enter into our circle once again, Child. We have come, for you have called. This gift we would like to give to all that wish to receive us. We have talked to them in meditation. We have talked to them on love and given to them our Father's wishes of peace on Earth. We have shared with them what must be done to protect our Mother Earth, the air we breathe, the water we drink, and the ground we plant our food in. We have shared with you many things such as death and life, happiness and sadness. What was and is now and what still can be. All that is needed is a better growth on your side. To open up to our father's wishes. To become what it is we all need to become. To hold your heads up high and take a stand. To be! What, you ask? We shall tell you. To be whole! To be one! To be connected once again. To reach out and find yourself. How many of you have asked yourselves this question. What am I going to be when I grow up? Don't be shocked for we hear it all the time. The want in your voices, the need to know what is going to happen. What are you going to do with your life? For many of you have no idea. Oh yes, you work, you do day to day activities. Yet, you know there is more. So much more. Yet, you know not what it is. You crave something and need something more. You know beyond a shadow of a doubt that there is more in store for you. There is more to your life than what you have now. But what? That is the question. One in which we have been sent here to answer. One in which we do very simply. One in which we let you know. We are here to help you. Help you what you ask. Help you to develop and become whole once again. There is a spiritual awakening. One in which all souls want to be heard. There is a trick here. One in which you are in control of. That is, you are the one who must realize this. You are the one who must agree to learn, to grow, to become and unite with the rest. You are the one that must consent. You and you alone have to pick up that book and read. You have to go to classes, start meditating, praying, communicating with us. Only then can we connect. Only then can we find that spot within to become whole once again. Only then child, can we become one. One with the universe; one with our father; one with ourselves once again. We have shared with you. We have walked you through simple phases. We have started you thinking in the ways in which one should think. We know you have already. If not, you would never have picked up our book. Your soul cries out to you. Stop, listen and know what it is you must do. Do! Yes, that is a hard word – big and powerful word. Nevertheless, you and only you can go forward. You can be and do anything at all that you wish to do. Can you? We just told you that you could. Now you have to make the next step. It waits for you. We wait for you. Your soul waits for you. Is it not time to know what you want to be when you grow up? We know! Do you? Grow child and let us help you in the most beautiful growth that could ever be. What you ask? There is only one answer for that. You!

*Love to you, my children. May the knowledge and wisdom seep into your lives like the breath of air you consume for your lungs. Let the beauty of our world connect with your world. That we may become one with each other.*

*Amen.*

Amen. What a beautiful prayer, Lizzy.

Yes, Child, one of truth.

You know, Lizzy, you always touch on something in my life. For many years, I knew I wanted more. Yet I did not know what. As you said, I used to laugh and say I wondered what I'm going to be or do when I grow up.

You know I hit my thirties and I'm still saying it. I hit my forties and something is not right. Just about one-half of my life is over and I still do not know what I'm going to be when I grow up. Oh, I worked and worked different jobs, schools, training programs to better myself. Yet, I still knew I was not fulfilled. Something was missing! I wanted more. Needed more. But what? Through a lot of this time, I would hear about a special book. Hear a story about a special person. Go to a psychic now and then. My world started to really open after I made an appointment with a medium who channeled. What is that you ask? I shall tell you. He speaks to the spirits. Your spirits. He helped me in my belief in my direction. I'll never forget my first visit to him. He said my father walked in behind me and kissed me on the cheek. Instant tears . He gave me a message to give to my mother. He helped me realize that there is so much more to life than this physical world. We have it all. We can have it all. I went to him about once a year. He is the spitting image of a wonderful grandfather type. Silver gray hair, kind eyes, wonderful smile and most of all, the love that shone from within him. You could wallow in it and be filled with all the love you could handle. Let me explain this to you. He never knew me. Only asked first names. He sees so many people a year you are like a stranger to him. It goes like this. You call to make an appointment and give your first name. You go into a precious little room for the readings. He sits in his chair and you sit in yours. No cards are needed. No music. His shelves are filled with books, bibles, and wonderful pictures. He starts to read for you. If you have any questions left at the end, he will answer them. He looks up into the air and speaks to your spirit guides. He will tell you who is with you. You can have many. Relatives, friends, or guides who work with you. Many are known to have Indian guides, doctors, writers, teachers, whatever, who ever. They walk with us. They help us. They make themselves known to you through him. It's amazing. Like a whole new world opening up. Scary? Absolutely not! Intriguing? Oh, yes! For they can help you. Explain to you and be there for you. This medium would pull out a book and tell me it was a wonderful book. I should read it. I thought, "Okay, I will." Every year I learned a little more. Started getting books a little by myself. Now I moved away. Out of state to Wisconsin. A small little town. Great for the kids to grow up in. Now they are grown. I feel lost. What do I do with my life now? I'm suffocating here. I wanted more. I didn't know what it was I wanted. I knew I could not find it there or in my marriage, as we had grown separate. We went our own way. Do I miss him? Yes, very much. He was a part of me for a very long time. My children's father, my husband, my friend. I knew I needed more. I had to take that step and then that step met with many others. I had to go through these steps to get to where I am today. Most of them were very hard steps for me and very personal ones and ones of growth for me and me alone. I had no one to share with. No one to understand what I was going through. I felt alone. Then when I felt I could not take another step alone, I traveled to Michigan where I met a gentle soul. He explained why we go through the things we do. He opened up my understanding of all that had happened. For these experiences have helped me to become the person I am now. We must go through changes in our lives in order to complete our tasks here on this Earth Plane. Whether good or bad, we must partake for growth. We do get to make the decision how we do it. So many of us want to know why! Yes, Why is a big question. What I can say to you is this. We come here to this Earth Plane for a purpose. One in which we have chosen to go through. One in which we must go through in order to complete our oneness. Again, it is up to you how you go through it, how you handle it, and how you grow from it. Going back to my story. I must say I have carried this guilt with me for many years. What guilt you wonder. The guilt of leaving my husband. The guilt of splitting the two of us. I have been told not to feel guilty. I had to do that in order to complete what it is I must do. Also, to help him complete what it is he has to do. Together it would never have happened. Now, we are on two separate paths of growth. He has found a new life of love and land. I have found a new life of spirituality and a path that keeps me going and growing beyond my wildest dreams. Are we both happy? I think so. Are our children happy? Yes, I think so. For you see with my growth, my children are growing, as are my grandchildren. What a gift. Did I have to work for it? Yes! Would I do it all over again? Yes! Will I continue to grow and blossom like that rose tree? I sure hope so! I must tell you this. When someone comes into your life and shares a book with you, a comment with you, a prayer with you, listen for these are gifts of our angels, guides, and teachers. Reaching out to let you know you are loved and being watched over. We all have teachers. Many, many teachers throughout our lives. My teacher is that very same silver-haired grandfather type medium that I previously told you about. He reached out to me and told me about his class and if I wanted to learn I was more than welcome to attend. He opened the door with an invitation. I accepted with a smile. Since the beginning of time, I always knew there was more. I never knew what. Now, I know what. God has sent his angel to me to teach me what it is I need to know, to grow and to become whole once again. With these few words, we hope we will be able to introduce you to our world of wonder, bliss, and oneness.

Our love to you all
Your friend and spirit guide,     Kathy & Liz

## ABOUT THE AUTHOR

Kathleen Marie Garbe-Modzelewski was born and raised in Detroit, Michigan. She is married to Michael, a wonderful spiritual man . His concern, love, and belief in her book has opened her heart and soul to him. Kathleen has three beautiful daughters, Lucinda, Tina and Christy and a handsome son Andy and a wonderful stepson Steven. She is the grandmother to four, her joy in life. Kathleen works in marketing and seeks pleasure in writing. Her greatest gift to share with her readers are the lessons she has learned through her Spirit Guides.